THE CITY OF WESTMINSTER

(Opposite title page)
Looking down Victoria Street
towards Westminster

THE CITY OF WESTMINSTER

A celebration of people and places

Photography by Alice Rosenbaum

Foreword by Simon Jenkins

Published in support of the Sir Simon Milton Foundation

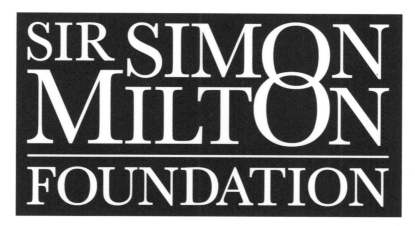

Charity Registration Number: 1149166

Quartet

First published in 2017 by Quartet Books Limited
A member of the Namara Group
27 Goodge Street, London W1T 2LD
Copyright © The Sir Simon Milton Foundation
Registered Charity Number: 1149166
www.sirsimonmiltonfoundation.com
Photographs © Alice Rosenbaum
Text © David Elliott
The right of the Sir Simon Milton Foundation to be identified
as the author of this work has been asserted
by them in accordance with the
Copyright, Designs and Patents Act, 1988.
All rights reserved.
No part of this book may be reproduced in
any form or by any means without prior
written permission from the publisher.
A catalogue record for this book
is available from the British Library.
ISBN 978 0 7043 7406 5
Typeset by Josh Bryson
Design by e-Digital Design
Printed and bound in Belgium by
DreckersSnoeck, Baarbeck, 2070 Zwijndrecht, Belgium

In memory of
Sir Simon Milton, politician,
born 2 October 1961; died 11 April 2011

The portrait bust in the entrance hall at Westminster City Hall

FOREWORD

Local government is the Cinderella of the public realm. Alternately abused and ignored, many of its institutions languish. Its achievements are nationalised while its services, in time of trouble, are first to be cut. This degeneration of the local is unique among democratic states. As a result, few distinguished men and women make local government the focus of their ambition. Gone are the days when the route to public service was through civic leadership.

Not so Simon Milton. His loyalty was to London in general and the city of his birth, Westminster, in particular. He served it as a councillor for twenty years, eight of them as council leader. He then spent three years working with London's mayor, Boris Johnson, before his untimely death. The reputation of the Westminster he took on in 2000 was tarnished. Milton swiftly removed that blemish. To him, city leadership was not about party advantage but about executive competence, about the prosperity and liveability of his environs.

Today Westminster is both the richest and most carefully guarded city-within-a-city in Europe. The virtuous circle between visual beauty and civic prosperity was understood by Milton, at a time when it was being abandoned by many surrounding boroughs. He guarded its inheritance of estates, squares and green spaces. Despite occasional lapses, Westminster under Milton respected the principle that civic dignity required constant protection from skyscraper intrusion and ugly development.

The continued popularity of Westminster for both businesses and residents was testament to Milton's success. He helped fashion a city that will probably remain much as he left it, at least for a very long time. He was a good custodian of the spirit of place and his monument, like Wren's, is to be seen on all sides.

Simon Jenkins

INTRODUCTION

Sir Simon Milton (right) and his civil partner, Cllr. Robert Davis MBE DL

The City of Westminster is one of the most unique and dynamic places in the world and for the past 34 years, variously as Councillor, Lord Mayor and Deputy Leader I have been fortunate enough to enjoy a front row seat to an astonishing degree of progress and growth. However, there is one moment which still stands out above all the rest.

That came in 1988 when a young man by the name of Simon Milton contacted me to discuss his wish to contest a by-election and join the Council. Over the next 23 years he became my partner in every sense, leaving a truly indelible mark on my life. Before his tragic death in 2011, Simon had become one of the most successful politicians in London's history. He served as Leader of Westminster City Council for what remains a record-breaking tenure between 2000 and 2008 and was Chairman of the Local Government Association from 2007-2008. Following Boris Johnson's election as Mayor of London in 2008, Simon stood down as Leader of Westminster Council to become his Deputy Mayor and Chief of Staff.

The Westminster City Council Crest by the entrance to City Hall

Simon was knighted in 2006 for his work in Westminster, in recognition of his pioneering 'One City' vision and the role he played in leading a grieving city in the aftermath of the 7/7 bombings. The 'One City' initiative was founded on Simon's firm belief that a place is truly the sum of its parts. Whether it is in providing young people with jobs and training, ensuring that older people are fully integrated into their communities, or creating a built environment that complements the city around it, no stone was left unturned in realising his ideas.

In 2012 a new charity was formed, the Sir Simon Milton Foundation, with one overriding aim – to continue delivering his vision of a caring City that offers opportunity for all. This book gives a snapshot of those many different aspects of Westminster's character, showing a year in the life of a city that never fails to astound and amaze. Even having served for more than three decades, I learn something new about this wonderful place each and every day, which I hope becomes clear in the pages you are about to turn.

Councillor Robert Davis MBE DL
Deputy Leader, Westminster City Council

1

The statistics alone are remarkable. Westminster's commercial economy makes up three per cent of the entire UK economy. Augmenting the 240,000 residents who already live there, over a million people come into the City of Westminster every day. Three of London's busiest railway stations are just one way for commuters to travel into what is now the largest employment centre in the United Kingdom, offering over 600,000 jobs in 43,000 businesses.

Westminster's West End has a monthly footfall of nearly 22 million. Westminster's 38 theatres help to generate, along with its cinemas, restaurants, bars and clubs, billions of pounds each year, making it one of most visited and successful entertainment centres in the world.

Westminster contains most of the offices of the British government, a fact recognised by the use of the name of one of its iconic streets – Whitehall – as a collective term given by the media to mean those who take part in any central government action or procedure: 'Whitehall said this,' or 'Whitehall did that.' Westminster Council is responsible for clearing the rubbish from the principal workplace of the monarch of the United Kingdom. Dustbins must also be emptied from the London residence of the heir to the throne, Clarence House, situated a little further down the Mall away from Buckingham Palace.

Westminster's architectural heritage, despite the terrible destruction of the blitz during World War Two, means that three-quarters

(Above) Though the smallest of Westminster's stations, Marylebone services the M40 corridor, Buckinghamshire, Oxfordshire, Warwickshire and the West Midlands

(Left) The evening rush hour at Victoria Station

(Below) Paddington Station was built in 1838, for all trains going west. It also runs a high-speed service to and from Heathrow airport

(Above left) Under the clock at Selfridges

(Above) Shoppers throng Oxford Street

(Left) Her Majesty's Theatre, Haymarket, where *Phantom of the Opera* first opened in 1986.

(Below) The statue of President Roosevelt, unveiled in 1948, looks over Grosvenor Square, while Mayfair office workers and Oxford Street shoppers enjoy a break in the summer sunshine

(Above) 'Big Ben' and the Palace of Westminster from Parliament Square

(Below) Whitehall, the Monument to the Women of World War Two with the Cenotaph in the distance, looking down to Parliament Square

of Westminster lies within a conservation area: The Palace of Westminster, the seat of government; Westminster Abbey, where our Kings and Queens were buried for nearly 900 years, and where our monarchs have been crowned ever since William I; the Cenotaph, the nation's symbol of remembrance and the focus of national attention on the eleventh hour of the eleventh day in the eleventh month and situated in the middle of Whitehall, the street that leads up to probably one of the most famous public spaces in the world, Trafalgar Square, which lies a few minutes' walk from the equally famous meeting place, Piccadilly Circus. It is said that you need only stand by Eros for less than an hour and you will always meet someone you know.

Yet Westminster stretches well beyond its centre, almost reaching Swiss Cottage to the north, curving along the Thames towards the

south, joining the tip of the City of London as the Strand meanders
into Fleet Street in the east and, in the west, it captures Knightsbridge
as its own from the jealous eyes of Kensington and Chelsea. No
wonder it boasts one of the largest number of listed buildings of any
borough in the land.

But amongst the historic districts and affluent residences, there are also
pockets of deprivation. And one of the realities of growing old in a major
city can be loneliness and isolation. The Sir Simon Milton Foundation
was set up with one overriding aim – to continue delivering Sir Simon's
vision of a caring city which offers opportunity for all.

Sir Simon Milton's successful political and business careers were
built in the City of Westminster. His father, a Jewish émigré who
fled persecution in Europe, had also seen the Milton family business
flourish in the same city and Sir Simon recognised that Westminster,
which was also his home, had given the Miltons the opportunities to
succeed in life.

Simon's obituary in the *Guardian* contained an interesting sentence: 'He
was an intelligent, calm and modest man whose influence on London
government will be felt for years to come.' Though this book's main
intent is to offer a snapshot of the variety and diversity of people living,
working or just visiting Westminster, and hopes to reflect all its range
and complexity, it also seeks to be a tribute to the vision and legacy of
Sir Simon Milton.

Peter Oborne's obituary of Sir Simon Milton in the *Daily Telegraph* sums
up the measure of what Simon achieved in such short a time. 'Very few
people knew about Sir Simon. But he was perhaps the most interesting,
quietly principled and far-sighted politician of his generation. Of
course, this makes his death all the more miserable. Enoch Powell's
famous observation that all political careers end in failure is very rarely
quoted in full. It reads as follows: "All political lives, unless they are cut
off in midstream at a happy juncture, end in failure, because that is the
nature of politics and of human affairs." Powell posted this observation
in his biography of Joseph Chamberlain. With one proviso – that he
was cut off cruelly at a very unhappy juncture – it applies very exactly
to Sir Simon Milton. Millions of Londoners will lead better and richer
lives because of his life of unstinting duty and service.'

And Peter Oborne's concluding reference to the Paddington Basin
development (which is where this celebration of Sir Simon Milton's

vision will begin) is a perfect example of that vision: 'Another major legacy was the Paddington Basin initiative — whereby a huge disused area of land around the station became one of the largest central London developments in decades. But it was economic growth with a heart: Milton set up a body called "Paddington First", to help ensure that the poorer residents of W2 and W9 obtained the jobs on the construction sites.'

Work began on draining the basin in 2000 with the ambition eventually to create two million square feet of offices, homes and shops surrounded by ambitious leisure facilities. The basin became home to a number of companies including the Head Office of Marks and Spencer who moved here, from Baker Street, in 2004.

Paddington Basin was originally where a branch of the Grand Junction Canal ended. The Regent's Canal opened in 1801, allowing goods and people a water-transport route from the Great Western Railway, and the industries of north London could reach the Midlands and beyond.

(Below) The new Paddington development across from Paddington Green

(Above) Merchant Square, in the heart of Paddington Basin

(Left) Bruce Denny's sculpture of Sir Simon Milton, placed in the centre of Merchant Square, was unveiled in 2014

(Overleaf) Eventually, grand houses were built along the canal giving the name 'Little Venice' to a stretch of water from Paddington up to Maida Vale

(Left) Ornament and architectural diversity sparkle around the whole development.

(Below) Houseboats moored next to family villas. The City of Westminster was one of the first councils to open towpaths to the public for recreational use

(Above) Randolph Avenue, in Little Venice, where Sir Simon Milton lived

(Right) The great actress Sarah Siddons sits on Paddington Green, looking across the Westway towards Paddington Basin, though she originally faced the now demolished Paddington Town Hall

(Overleaf) Westminster, looking North from the roof of City Hall

2

Westminster City Council is a London borough council, granted the right by royal charter to be called a 'city council', a rare distinction in the United Kingdom. Westminster's history can be traced back over 1,000 years to when King Edward the Confessor ordered the rebuilding of a church which came to be called Westminster Abbey. He moved his palace to a site adjacent to the Abbey and called it the Palace of Westminster.

(Right) The 16th century Chapel of Henry VII

(Overleaf) The Henry VII chapel is a superb example of late Perpendicular architecture with a profusion of rich sculptured decoration and beautiful fan vaulting

(Left) Leaving Westminster Abbey after the annual Remembrance Sunday service

The hamlet, serving both the Abbey and the Palace of Westminster, grew through the Middle Ages into a vibrant town. As a consequence of the Great Fire of London Westminster developed even more, as those who could afford to rebuilt their homes around the Abbey and the Palace. When these grand homes and their large grounds became too big and too expensive to maintain, the landowners started granting leases of parts of their estates to developers. Even today, a large part of Westminster remains in the ownership of just a few families such as the Duke of Westminster, Viscount Portman and the De Walden family.

Queen Elizabeth I granted city status to Westminster, but refused to allow it to have its own independent City Council and Mayor as she thought an independent council would be a rival to her court. By an Act of Parliament of 1585, the responsibility for civic administration was vested in the Dean and Chapter of Westminster Abbey who in turn delegated the responsibility to a Court of Burgesses appointed by the Dean.

This arrangement continued until 1900 when it was eventually accepted that the residents of Westminster needed to elect their own City Council and in turn, the council would elect its own Mayor.

The city is now divided into 20 wards, each electing three councillors. The council was created by the London Government Act 1965, replacing three local authorities: Paddington Metropolitan Borough Council, St Marylebone Metropolitan Borough Council and Westminster City Council.

(Below) The mace is carried down and the Lord Mayor calls the meeting to order. The 60 council members meet temporarily in Porchester Hall whilst the City Council Chamber in Marylebone Road is being renovated

(Right) The City Council in session

(Below right) Members of the public can sit at the back of the hall to follow the proceedings

(Left) Tim Keech, the Westminster Waterman, and Paul Devine, one of the Macebearers, photographed in the Lord Mayor's Parlour, with a chiming clock modelled on Westminster Abbey in the background. Both will accompany the Lord Mayor in processions and at other civic functions, though the ceremonial oar no longer has any practical use. It is kept however, along with a number of maces, in the Plate Room at City Hall, which also houses the ceremonial gold and silver accumulated over the years alongside many gifts given to the City of Westminster by foreign dignitaries

(Right and below) The Westminster Tobacco Box is owned by the Past Overseers' Society of St. Margaret's and St. John's, Westminster, which took responsibility for the operations of the poor laws and running the workhouses within those parishes. Formed in the 18th century, they created a series of objects which had engraved on them two or three important events that happened within the city or the wider world each year since its inception in 1713

(Previous) The Lord Mayor welcomes the participants in the Lord Mayor's Parlour. Over 20,000 new citizens have chosen Westminster as their new home in recent years

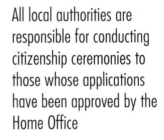

All local authorities are responsible for conducting citizenship ceremonies to those whose applications have been approved by the Home Office

Applicants make on oath of allegiance to HM The Queen and pledge to respect the rights, freedoms and laws of the United Kingdom

The main offices of the government of the United Kingdom are mostly located in the heart of Westminster. To stand on the bridge in St James's Park and look down to Buckingham Palace or up towards the magical turrets of Horse Guards and Whitehall is to witness a state architecture which is, for many, one of the finest in the world.

(Above) Towards the Italianate turrets of Whitehall
(Overleaf) Buckingham Palace
(Below) Visitors in St. James's Park snapping the view across to Whitehall

Alex Aiken is the Executive Director for Government Communications. One of the Cabinet Office's senior management team, he is responsible for government communication strategy. He worked closely with Sir Simon Milton as Director of Communications and Strategy for Westminster City Council

Nick Boles, MP for Grantham and Stamford, photographed in St Stephen's Yard in the Palace of Westminster, with Portcullis House on his right. A colleague of Sir Simon Milton, he was elected onto Westminster Council in 1998, becoming Chairman of Housing. Whilst the Minister of State for Education and Skills, he supported the creation of The Sir Simon Milton Westminster University Technical College (*see pages 145–146*)

The Rt. Hon. Greg Clark MP was a councillor on Westminster City Council, serving in Sir Simon Milton's cabinet as its member for Leisure and Lifelong Learning. He is currently Secretary of State for Business, Energy and Industrial Strategy

Photographed near the Peers' Entrance to the House of Lords, Baroness Margaret Eaton, DBE DL was Leader of Bradford Metropolitan Borough Council for many years, served as Leader of the Conservative Group during Simon Milton's tenure as Chairman of the Local Government Association and succeeded him as Chairman. Her long friendship with and admiration for Sir Simon Milton is celebrated in her role as a Trustee of the Sir Simon Milton Foundation

It is only natural that embassies and high commissions wish to be near the seat of government and Westminster has more than its fair share. One of the most impressive, Canada House, stands along the entire west side of Trafalgar Square. Built in 1827, designed by Sir Robert Smirke (the architect of the British Museum), it was bought by the Canadian government in 1923. The renovated building was officially opened on 29 June 1925 by King George V. A major renovation began in 2014, bringing together all the High Commission's diplomatic functions under one roof, including a gallery to stage exhibitions of historical and contemporary art and artefacts.

(Above) Gordon Campbell, OBC, was Canada's High Commissioner to the United Kingdom from 2011–2016. He served three terms as Premier of the province of British Columbia. Mr Campbell began his political career in Vancouver and served as its Mayor for three successive terms

(Left) Trafalgar Square photographed from the roof of Canada House. Taken a few days after Remembrance Sunday, poppies still linger in the fountains

(Right) The Bee Hotel on the roof of Canada House, provided by the Canadian owners of the Savoy. Canada House honey will be served with tea if the bees flourish

(Overleaf) The Strand entrance to the Savoy Hotel, one of the world's legendary luxury hotels

3

One of Europe's largest railway and infrastructure construction projects, Crossrail is a 73-mile (118-kilometre) railway line, begun in 2009 with the excavation of a new tunnel underneath central London. Connections to existing lines which will become part of Crossrail, link stations as far west as Reading, Shenfield in the north east and Abbey Wood in the south east. It will connect with Heathrow and branch from Whitechapel to Canary Wharf. Nine-carriage air-conditioned trains will run at frequencies of up to 24 trains per hour in each direction through the central section. The line will be called the Elizabeth Line, named after the world's longest serving monarch when it becomes operational through central London in 2018.

A ventilation shaft under construction for Bond Street station

The Crossrail building
site at Hanover Square
and an entrance for the
construction workers

Under Bond Street

Completing what will
become a platform at
Bond Street

(Above) Looking down what will become the platform at Bond Street

(Left) Sir Terry Morgan CBE took over the role of Chairman of Crossrail on 1 June 2009. He had been Chief Executive of Tube Lines, contracted to maintain and upgrade the infrastructure of the Jubilee, Northern and Piccadilly lines. He has an MSc in Engineering Production & Management, is a Fellow of the Royal Academy of Engineering and the Institute of Electrical Engineers and is the past President of the CMI (Chartered Management Institute)

(Right) Future walkways onto the Bond Street platform

Another major re-development is Nova, a site built by Land Securities opposite Victoria Station, which will name the new public space at its heart 'Sir Simon Milton Square' in recognition of his role in enabling the project to proceed (see pages 54-55). When completed in early 2017, Nova will offer 630,000 square feet of offices and 170 private apartments. It will boast a new restaurant quarter – 85,000 square feet with space for food markets, outdoor events, over 400 al fresco seats and 18 restaurants.

Completing the private apartments. Every unit comes ready made with fixtures and built-in fittings and each unit can simply be 'slotted' into their correct position, rather like using a massive Lego building kit

The next shift arrives

A party of visitors wait across from the site's main entrance

Colette O'Shea joined Land Securities in 2003 and was Head of Development, London Portfolio, before being appointed its Managing Director in April 2014. She has responsibility for Land Securities' £7.8bn London Portfolio comprising some nine million square foot of London offices, leisure, retail and residential property both in development and asset management. Colette is President of the British Council for Offices and a non-executive director of Genesis Housing Association

(Overleaf) This space will become the Sir Simon Milton Square, with trees, lawns and public spaces to be enjoyed

(Left) Colette and colleagues look out from the 17th floor of Nova South

(Overleaf) The show still goes on as Nova South grows ever upwards

A previous colossal engineering endeavour in Westminster had been the construction of Portcullis House, the new building across from the Palace of Westminster, above the reconstructed Westminster Underground station, enabling the new Jubilee Line to link up to the District and Circle lines. Designed by Hopkins Architects and completed in 1999, the station design won Civic Trust awards in 2000 and 2002, the Royal Fine Art Commission Millennium Building of the Year award in 2000, and the RIBA Award for Architecture in 2001

The District and Circle lines cut across the site at an angle of 45 degrees. This had a major influence on both the planning and the structure. All elements such as walls, escalators and ticket barriers follow either the diagonal grid of the railway or the orthogonal grid of the building above. The escalators to and from the Jubilee Line lie within a huge box of rough concrete, framed by a massive diagrid of beams and buttresses, which also form the foundations of Portcullis House

(Overleaf) The Jubilee Line was dug far deeper than the shallow District and Circle lines. The construction of a new Parliamentary building above them required a complex interchange to cope with the depth and axis of the lines, the positioning of the support for Portcullis House and excavation's proximity to Big Ben and the River Thames

4

Westminster houses a myriad of world faiths. The Collegiate Church of St Peter Westminster, better known as Westminster Abbey, is one of the world's iconic churches and certainly one of the most visited tourist spots in London. Few know it is a Royal Peculiar, a church exempt from the jurisdiction of the Church of England diocese in which it lies. It is subject to the direct jurisdiction of the monarch. And how many tourists notice, just across from the Abbey's Great West Door, the looming glory of Methodist Central Hall, completed in 1912 with funds sought by public subscription to celebrate the centenary of John Wesley's death, built upon the remains of an aquarium and music hall? And even fewer people could recall its role as host to the first ever meeting of the United Nations in 1946, though there is a commemorative plaque near its main entrance.

The Very Reverend Dr John Hall was installed as the 38th Dean of Westminster on 2 December 2006. The Dean oversees the spiritual life of and gives leadership to the Abbey community, which includes 300 staff and 500 volunteers. Since the Abbey is a Royal Peculiar, the Dean is responsible to the Sovereign alone.

(Right) The Dean is standing before the shrine of St. Edward the Confessor, Westminster Abbey's founder, east of the Sanctuary and at the heart of the Abbey

(Below) The Methodist Central Hall

He worked in Westminster from 1998 as the Church of England's Chief Education Officer, with overall responsibility for the Church's strategy, policy and practice in relation to schools. As Dean of Westminster he chairs the governors of Westminster School and Westminster Abbey Choir School. He also chairs the governors of Harris Westminster Sixth Form, a free school opened in Westminster in September 2014. A trustee of various charities and a holder of many honorary degrees and fellowships, Dr Hall became a Fellow of the Society of Antiquaries and was awarded the honorary degree of Doctor of Letters by the University of Westminster in 2014.

The London Central Mosque, situated in Regent's Park, is joined to the Islamic Cultural Centre. The Cultural Centre was opened by HM King George VI in 1944 built on land which the Churchill government gave in recognition of the considerable sacrifices made by Muslim troops during the Second World War. The beautiful mosque was not completed until 1978, designed by Sir Frederick Gibberd, well known for his Modernist structures including the Catholic cathedral in Liverpool. The Mosque has a prominent golden dome. The main hall can hold over five thousand with space for a further three thousand in the courtyard at times of the great festivals. The mosque houses a chandelier and a vast carpet, with very little furniture. The inside of the dome is decorated with broken shapes in the Islamic tradition.

(Right) Dr Ahmad Al-Dubayan is the Director General of the Islamic Cultural Centre. He worked as Head of the Research and Translation Unit at the Institute of Islamic and Arabic Studies in Jakarta from 1988 to 1990. Formerly, he was a lecturer in Arabic at the University of Imam and University of Indonesia in Jakarta

(Below left) The golden dome and the minaret on the edge of Regent's Park

(Below right) The chandelier in full glory

The West London Synagogue is a Reform Jewish synagogue, established on 15 April 1840. Its current building in Upper Berkeley Street dates from 1870, making it the oldest Reform synagogue that is still standing, and one of the oldest synagogues in the United Kingdom. The main sanctuary is built in the Neo-Byzantine architectural style by Davis & Emmanuel, though its premises, which extend into Seymour Place, also contain offices, a library and various community facilities. Sir Simon Milton was a member of this synagogue.

(Right) Rabbi Baroness Julia Neuberger DBE has been Senior Rabbi at West London Synagogue since 2011. She became a life peer in 2004 (as a Liberal Democrat, but is now a Cross Bencher)

The stained glass windows above the balcony

The Cathedral Church of Westminster was designed in the Early Christian Byzantine style by the Victorian architect John Francis Bentley. The foundation stone was laid in 1895 and the fabric of the building was completed eight years later

The interior of the Cathedral is still incomplete, but contains fine marble-work and mosaics, including carvings of the fourteen Stations of the Cross, by the sculptor Eric Gill

(Right) Vincent Gerard Nichols is an English Cardinal of the Roman Catholic Church, Archbishop of Westminster and President of the Catholic Bishops' Conference of England and Wales. He previously served as Archbishop of Birmingham from 2000 to 2009. Vincent Nichols was installed as the 11th Archbishop of Westminster in May 2009

(Above) Westminster Coroner's Court, on Horseferry Road, is a Grade II listed building and was built in 1893

(Left) Her Majesty's Coroner for Inner West London is Dr Fiona Wilcox, photographed here in the Horseferry Road court building. The coroner is responsible for inquisitions into sudden or suspicious deaths

(Left) The Honorary Recorder of Westminster, Judge Alistair McCreath, presides at the Crown Court situated in the Borough of Southwark. Westminster has no Crown Court within its boundaries and the cases which have their origin in Westminster are tried at Southwark Crown Court. The Recordership of Westminster creates a linkage between the City and the Court. The Recorder is appointed by the City Council

(Left) The smallest police station in Great Britain was created in 1926, made from a hollowed-out lamp post, it was installed so police could keep a close eye on demonstrators in Trafalgar Square, a major venue for popular protest. It had a direct line to Scotland Yard, though officials never confirmed this. It is no longer used, apart from the notice board which displays the by-laws for public gatherings in the square

(Right) Chief Superintendent Peter Ayling is Borough Commander of the City of Westminster and OCU (Operational Command Unit) Commander Royal Parks. He has responsibility for the day to day delivery of policing operations in Westminster, and the nearly 1,500 men and women who carry out that task

(Overleaf) Members of the Honourable Corps of Gentlemen at Arms emerge from Gieves & Hawkes to board their coach prior to providing a Guard of Honour for Her Majesty The Queen and the President of China at Buckingham Palace

73

The Queen's 90th birthday was celebrated on April 21 2016, in London with a 41 gun Royal Salute, fired at midday in Hyde Park by the King's Troop, Royal Horse Artillery. The King's Troop is a ceremonial unit of the British Army. It is mounted and all its soldiers, although available for operations around the world, are trained to care for and drive teams of six horses each pulling six First World War 13-pounder field guns. It is the most gender diverse unit in the British army and is most often seen providing gun salutes on state occasions in two of the city's great parks, Hyde Park and Green Park.

(Above) Final preparations at Wellington Barracks

(Below left) The horses are brought onto the parade ground and made ready for inspection

(Below right) The Band marches out first

(Left) The Troop leaves the barracks in procession to Hyde Park

(Middle left) The Troop gallop down from Marble Arch onto their firing positions

(Lower left) Firing commences. The standard Royal Salute is 21 rounds. In Hyde Park and Green Park an extra 20 rounds are added because they are Royal Parks

(Below) Back to barracks

5

The Notting Hill Carnival has taken place over the August Bank Holiday weekend for the past 50 years. Its route passes through both the City of Westminster and the Royal Borough of Kensington and Chelsea and both local authorities work with the Carnival organisers and others to ensure that the four-day festivity takes place with the minimum of disruption. It is not without controversy. Interviewed by BBC Radio London during the 2015 Carnival, the former Mayor of London, Boris Johnson, was concerned but recognised that 'it's the biggest street festival in the world outside Rio de Janeiro, it's been going for years, it's a great symbol of London's culture and it generates a huge amount of revenue for the city.' It is also the responsibility of the two local authorities to spend over £500,000 on provision for public toilets and the cost of the clean-up operation when the party's over.

(Previous, below and right) The 2015 event was plagued by almost continual rain. The Monday Parade and Grand Finale showcased a sea of vibrant colours as 60 bands in magnificent costumes danced to the tantalizing rhythms of mobile sound systems and steel bands. Everyone — even the police — did their best despite the weather

(Right) Bedraggled, but determined to finish the route

The BBC Proms, or using their more formal title, The Henry Wood Promenade Concerts, are an eight-week summer season of daily classical music concerts, held annually, mostly in the Royal Albert Hall, with every concert broadcast on BBC Radio 3. Founded in 1895, the last concert of the season has become over the years a traditional mixture of culture and chaos. Seats are subject to lottery, the event is broadcast in over 70 countries, and is an especially British oddity, with rowdy singing of nationalistic fervour, much stamping of feet and frantic flag-waving. 'The Last Night of the Proms' was extended by the BBC into four events entitled 'Proms in the Park' with musical high jinks organised in Belfast, Glasgow, Swansea and London's Hyde Park, just east of the Royal Albert Hall, between the Serpentine and Park Lane.

Westminster Council has the responsibility, alongside the Royal Parks, to ensure good order, the minimum of inconvenience to local residents and assists in keeping concert-goers in a safe environment. It is a strange, rather wonderful mixture of a traditional seaside bandstand, brash rock concert and a somewhat delinquent Glyndebourne picnic. The 2015 highlight was conductor Marin Alsop, the BBC Symphony Orchestra and the massed audiences of four public parks performing *Do Re Mi* from *The Sound of Music*.

(Below) The audience aim to find their 'spot' early, but the empty bins are already in position

(Right) Time for tea?

(Below right) A pre-concert sing-a-long warm-up for *Do Re Mi*

(Overleaf) Alison Balsom plays Haydn

(Above) Stewards mingle with the waiting crowds   (Below) Waiting for the next announcement

London Fashion Week is held in February and September. Organised by the British Fashion Council, it has become on a par with the fashion weeks held in New York, Paris and Milan, since it first took place in 1984. Although a trade event, it attracts significant press attention. Attended by over 5,000 media professionals and retail buyers, it has estimated orders as high as £100 million.

The September 2015 event was held for the first time in the art deco car park on Brewer Street in the heart of Soho. The rain did little to dampen the enthusiasm.

(Above) The Brewer Street car park has hosted exhibitions, 'happenings' and many other events since 2002, although it still functions as a car park from its lower ground floor

(Below) The trade exhibition on the second floor, above the catwalk shows held below on the first

(Above) The ubiquitous media

(Below) The weather doesn't stop the show

6

Silver Sunday, held on the first Sunday in October, is an annual day of fun and free activities for older people organised across the UK. Championed by one of the Sir Simon Milton Foundation Trustees, Christabel Flight, it celebrates the value and knowledge the elderly contribute to our communities while combating loneliness and isolation. Silver Sunday 2016 was the most successful so far with well over 600 free events and activities taking place across the UK, attended by thousands of older people. Westminster alone offered over 50 events. The aim is for Silver Sunday to become a national day on a par with Fathers' Day and Mothering Sunday.

(Below) Under instruction on Silver Sunday in the gym at the Porchester Spa

(Overleaf) Swimming on Silver Sunday at the Porchester Baths

(Above) The Lord Mayor instigates the Silver Sunday cricket match at Lords

(Below) The game begins under the Media Centre

(Overleaf) The iconic Pavilion at Lords, now a grade II listed building

(Right) Participants in the Wallace Collection Silver Sunday activity session

(Below) A point is explained at the Wallace Collection

(Above) Silver Sunday ends with a sing-along in the Lord Mayor's Parlour

(Left) Everyone can get involved, whether that's organising an event, spreading the word, or simply attending an activity

(Above) Cllr. The Baroness Couttie of Downe, Leader of Westminster Council, welcomes the guests

Councillor The Lady Flight instigated the annual Christmas Tea Dance (held in the Great Room of the Grosvenor Hotel in Park Lane) under Simon Milton's leadership. Now in its tenth year, the Tea Dance is a free event for 1,000 Westminster residents aged 65 or more who apply for tickets. Many participants attend regularly, making new friendships and renewing old ones. The Christmas Tea Dance has become one of the main events in the Sir Simon Milton Foundation's calendar.

The 2015 Tea Dance saw Joanna Lumley invited as a very special guest. She had attended the very first event ten years earlier.

(Right) The old tunes are the best!

(Above) The band begins to rock   (Below) The dance floor gets crowded

The Lord Mayor and Joanna Lumley made sure every table had the chance to meet them

(Right) Second helpings?

(Below) Selfies all round

The Westminster Almshouses Foundation is responsible for thirty-eight flats; each has a sitting-room, bedroom, kitchen and bathroom. Tenants must have a clear residential connection with Westminster and be able to look after themselves. Many of the present buildings date from 1879 when all the various Westminster almshouses, some dating back to 1656, were consolidated here in Rochester Row.

(Above) Each building divides into flats

(Left) Anyone for any more?

(Above) The residents participate in Macmillan Cancer's Biggest Coffee Morning

(Right) All the cakes and biscuits were baked by the residents

(Left) Replete

(Below) Cllr. Susie Burbridge was Simon Milton's fellow Ward Councillor in the Lancaster Gate Ward from 2002–2008. She worked in Parliament for many years and organised the first plaque dedicated to a woman in the House of Commons, Marjorie Hume, a suffragette in the long battle to get women the vote

Alice photographed outside the Sherlock Holmes Museum, near where she works. During the year many thousands of adoring fans of the great detective visit his fictional home, just a few hundred yards from that other huge tourist attraction, Madam Tussauds

The Westminster Community Awards are judged and given by Westminster Council each year and recognise 'the local heroes' who dedicate their time to benefit the lives of others in the community.

Alice Caffyn won her Young Volunteer award in 2014. She volunteered with the befriending services run by the Octavia Foundation for lonely older people after reading an article in *The Reporter*, the council's resident magazine.

The Inspiration Award is awarded to individuals who have overcome obstacles or gone beyond the call of duty to benefit a voluntary organisation or cause. Brenda Meadows won in 2014. She is an active member of the community and works quietly to improve both individual lives and the community by her involvement in the local Scout, Beaver and Cub groups, the community market and with the Out and About Club.

Brenda in front of the community stall at the Maida Hill Market on the Harrow Road. All proceeds from the stall go to help community activities

Three winners from 2014 photographed in front of the Suffragette Scroll, just across from Caxton Hall. Jonathan Drake-Wilkes won the Active Volunteer Award for his work with local rowing clubs; on his right, Zoe Smith, a swimmer, was Champion of the Future and Lucy Mellers won the London Youth Games Award

The Active Westminster Awards celebrate the contribution of individuals and clubs who make a difference through sport and physical activity. Now in their sixth year, the awards are a chance to highlight the hard work of inspiring people and organisations across Westminster.

The Sir Simon Milton Foundation gives scholarships to students from Westminster with disadvantaged backgrounds to help them into and through university. Meheret Hddisalem, one of the current Sir Simon Milton Scholars who was originally in the Council's care, is now at Kingston University reading Civil Engineering. She is photographed beside Yinka Shoibare's *Wind Sculpture* in Howick Place, Victoria, with Maj. Gen. Matthew Sykes CVO, Chief Executive of the Sir Simon Milton Foundation

The Sir Simon Milton Award is given annually to recognise those working with older people or the disadvantaged young. Jane Buchanan, the 2016 awardee (for her volunteer work at St John's Hospice), stands by the *Tree of Life* in the Hospice's reception area, located within the Hospital of St John and St Elizabeth in St John's Wood. This independent charity provides specialised palliative care to more than 3,000 terminally-ill patients and their families every year

7

The Suffragette Scroll is just one example of sculptures commemorating the gaining of female suffrage. A quick walk from their Scroll, down Victoria Street, past the Palace of Westminster and tucked in a corner just by the entrance to the House of Lords stands a 1930 statue of the suffragette's leader, Emmeline Pankhurst

(Below) The Buxton Memorial Fountain commemorates the emancipation of slaves in the British Empire, commissioned by Charles Buxton MP, and dedicated to his father, along with all who had been involved in the abolition movement. Completed in 1866, it stood in Parliament Square till it was removed in 1949. Reinstated in Victoria Tower Gardens in 1957, it was restored in 2007 as part of the commemoration of the 200th anniversary of the Act to abolish the slave trade

(Left) Shaftesbury Avenue
–'Theatreland'– lights up for
its night-time performances

(Right) Cllr. Robert Davis
MBE DL has served as a
Councillor on Westminster City
Council for over 34 years and
was Lord Mayor in 1996.
Currently Deputy Leader of the
Council and Cabinet Member
for the Built Environment
with specific responsibility
for Planning, the Mayoralty
and City Promotions, his
portfolio also covers Public
Art. He is photographed with
one of the sculptures from
the old glockenspiel that
used to play around the now
demolished Swiss Centre on
Leicester Square

(Below) Councillor Davis was responsible for a mini-version of the original glockenspiel which he unveiled just across from its old home in 2011

Eran Akerman, CEO of the Halycon Gallery, standing by *She Guardian* by Dashi Namdakov, at Marble Arch. The Halcyon Gallery has displayed a long-standing passion for philanthropy and public placements, with the firm belief that art should be accessible to everyone. The sculpture was unveiled in May 2015 as part of Westminster's City of Sculpture programme. Westminster boasts over 400 public sculptures, more than any other town or city in the UK

Dunamis by Bushra Fakhoury, a British sculptor, born in Lebanon. The Greek word for 'power', *Dunamis* is a 9 metre tall sculpture standing near Hyde Park Corner on a traffic island in Park Lane

A major special event is the annual New Year's Day Parade which celebrated its 30th year in 2015. Each London Borough competes with individual floats, mixed up with American marching bands, helium-filled balloons, horses and bagpipes – over 60 entrants.

(Above) The Lord Mayor's Landau gets ready to lead the parade as the Mace is passed up

(Below) The London Mayors greet the crowds from an open-top bus

(Above) The Varsity All American Cheerleaders, Dancers and Spirit Performers get ready

(Below) The Wizard balloon, with his apprentices from Oklahoma

(Right) The Edna Karr Marching Band from New Orleans

(Left) Nica Burns, OBE, is a London theatre producer, Chief Executive and co-owner, with her business partner Max Weitzenhoffer, of the Nimax Theatres group, which owns six London theatres. The Garrick, just across from Leicester Square at the bottom of Charing Cross Road, opened in 1889. Its antiquated facilities meant that every new production required the carrying in of an entire stage set and equipment through the front of house and down a narrow staircase into the stalls, as the door for the set was not big enough for anything other than rolled up canvas backdrops. When Kenneth Branagh's Theatre Company wanted to take the Garrick for a year to run a repertory season, Nimax decided a complete refit was required. Remarkably, in five weeks, the somewhat dilapidated theatre was transformed. A new backstage area with state of the art facilities and a brand new door with a bespoke lift was installed, which could allow scenery and equipment to be easily unloaded into the right place at the right moment

A shot from dress circle level, with a corner of *The Winter's Tale* set, designed by Christopher Oram for the Kenneth Branagh Theatre Company

(Above left) A corner of the refurbished Gold Bar on the first floor

(Below) The sign every actor loves

(Above right) The main chandelier and dome high above the stalls

(Right) Nica Burns OBE, Dame Judi Dench and Sir Kenneth Branagh, photographed shortly before a matinee of *The Winter's Tale*. The actors have just finished their pre-performance on-stage warmup

(Left) Photographed in its front stalls, Alex Beard CBE is Chief Executive of the Royal Opera House, Covent Garden. At the end of 2012 he was appointed a CBE for his services to the arts

(Right) Julian Bird, Chief Executive, and Emma De Souza, Head of Media & Marketing from the Society of London Theatre (SOLT), photographed outside the TKTS official London Theatre ticket booth in Leicester Square. SOLT also produce the annual Olivier Awards and co-produce West End Live with Westminster

(Below left) The Royal Opera House is one of the top opera venues in the world. The National Lottery awarded it £58.5m. towards re-building costs and in 1990, at a total cost of £178m., the theatre was utterly transformed

(Right) Bar Italia on Frith Street, one of the few fixed points in an ever-evolving Soho, was opened in 1949 by Luigi and Caterina Polledri. Their grandchildren continue to run the show and the bar is still open 22 hours a day

(Overleaf) Covent Garden borders Soho, an area long famed for its louche, bohemian atmosphere. Striptease still settles happily amongst National Theatre productions

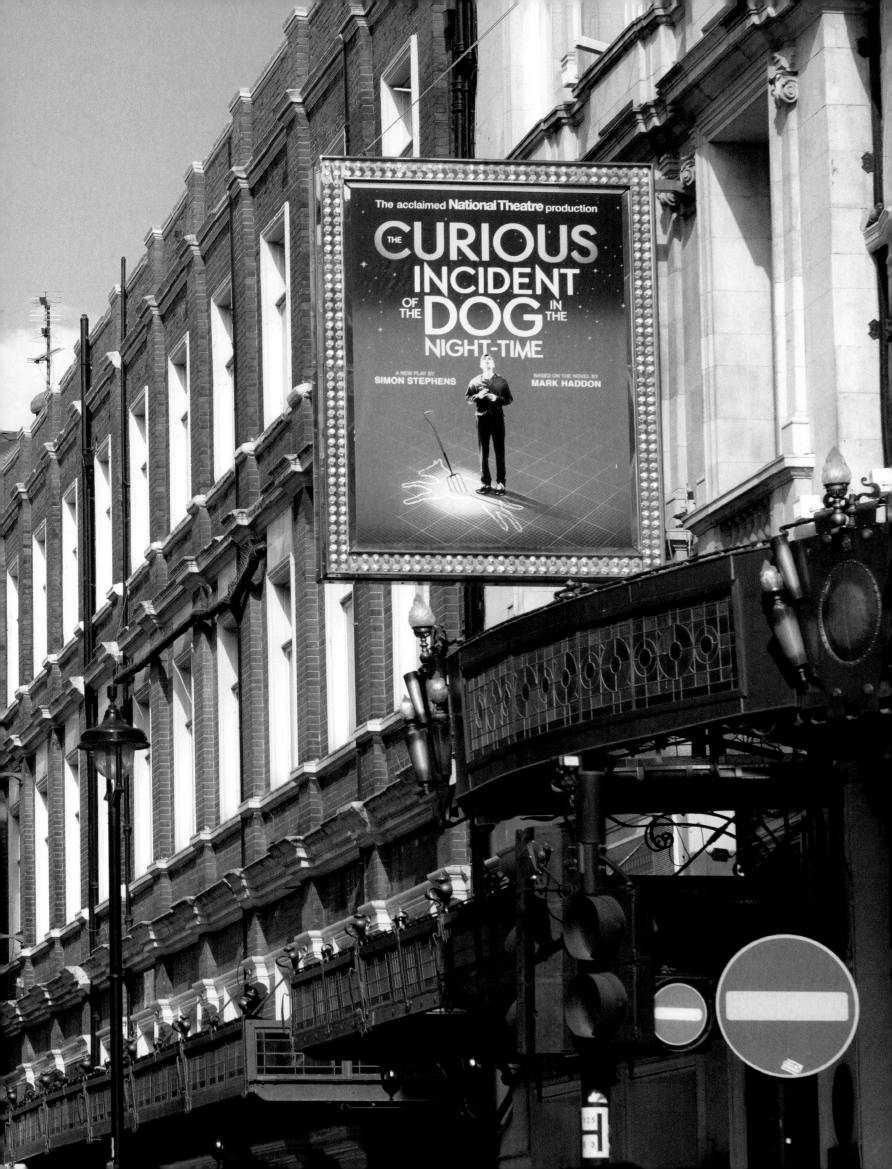

(Above) Cllr. Robert Davis MBE DL and Julia Corkey, Director of Strategy and Communications at the City of Westminster, (seated) both trustees of the Sir Simon Milton Foundation, planning the next *West End Live*, the annual summer weekend bonanza when highlights from West End musicals are performed for free in Trafalgar Square, with Richie Gibson and Kim Patterson, the event organisers. The large photograph of the musical *Jersey Boys* being performed there is on the back wall of Councillor Davis's City Hall office

(Right) Simon Thomas, above the ground floor gaming tables. There are four floors of gaming including a Gold Room casino with access directly into Chinatown to the rear of the building, a restaurant, six bars, a smoking terrace and The Matcham Room cabaret theatre. In January 2013 the casino was awarded Best Land-based Casino at the Totally Gaming Awards

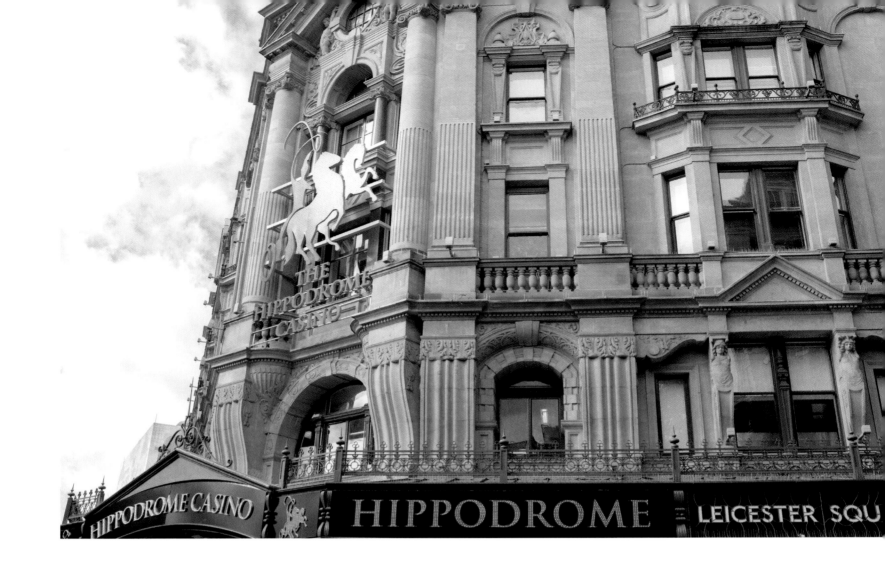

(Above) The Hippodrome has been synonymous with innovation and stylish entertainment since it was first opened in 1900. Designed by the great theatre architect Frank Matcham originally as a venue for circus and variety performances, it was reconstructed in 1909 as a variety theatre. Extraordinary entertainment made the Hippodrome famous. It hosted the UK's first jazz performance, the debut of Tchaikovsky's *Swan Lake* and some of Harry Houdini's most spectacular acts. In 1957 the London Hippodrome was converted into the nightclub, The Talk of the Town. In February 1964, Ethel Merman made her only British appearance in a season of cabaret. In 2009, the lease on the Hippodrome was acquired by Leicester-born father-and-son entrepreneurs Jimmy and Simon Thomas, who began an extensive £40m. restoration programme taking the Hippodrome back to Matcham's original designs for use as a casino and entertainment venue. The Hippodrome Casino was opened on 13 July 2012 by Councillor Robert Davis and the then Mayor of London, Boris Johnson, who described it as 'yet another ringing endorsement of London as a great place to invest'

8

The management and maintenance of Westminster's very valuable real estate is a delicate negotiation between maintaining the often historic original buildings yet ensuring a vibrant, modern approach to any necessary re-development.

Shaftesbury is a Real Estate Investment Trust, which owns a portfolio extending to 14 acres in the heart of Westminster.

(Above right, from left to right) Tom Welton, Brian Bickell and Simon Quayle on the roof of Shaftesbury's Soho offices. Brian is Chief Executive; Tom, an Executive director with responsibility for the portfolio of properties in Chinatown and Covent Garden, and Simon, Executive Director with responsibility for properties in Carnaby, Soho and Charlotte Street

(Right) David Shaw OBE is responsible for the Crown Estate's Regent Street portfolio and is photographed at the top end of the street, looking down towards Piccadilly. The Christmas lights are being strung across in preparation for the festive season. The revenues from the Crown Estate were placed by the monarch at the disposition of the British government for the benefit of the nation. Its London portfolio includes the entirety of Regent Street and around half of the area of St. James's, on the south side of Piccadilly. Since 2002, when David joined the Crown Estate, the 4 million square feet portfolio has undergone a wholesale transformation

A nearby panel gives the mural's provenance:

'The Spirit of Soho mural was created by the Soho community and completed in 1991. It shows Soho life and is dedicated to the people of Soho. The mural depicts St Anne presiding over local notables; her skirt and petticoats show the map of Soho, craftsmen and London landmarks. Framed underneath are the portraits of Soho's many famous figures. Dogs and hares are interspersed which represent a time when Soho was a Royal hunting ground. Restored in 2006 by Shaftesbury PLC and The Soho Society, the clock was re-activated by The Lord Mayor of Westminster on October 19 2006. Don't miss: When the clock strikes on the hour, watch actress and opera singer Theresa Cornelys wink at Casanova, Casanova blows a series of kisses to Cornelys and Karl Marx takes a sip of Coca Cola.'

(Above) Covent Garden, looking down across the West Piazza, in front of the renovated Market Building. 69 per cent of visitors to London choose to visit Covent Garden specifically and it is estimated there are 42 million customer visits every year

(Right) Sarah-Jane Curtis, who until summer 2016 was a Director of Capital & Counties Properties PLC (Capco) and responsible for the Covent Garden estate. Capco made the first major purchase of the Covent Garden Estate in 2006. Since then they have spearheaded its transformation by bringing in a host of innovative global brands as well as offering a wide range of culinary experiences

(Above) Given Covent Garden's history of involvement with culture and the arts, special events are encouraged. Here, the French artist Charles Pétillon filled the Market Building with an installation of 100,000 white balloons

(Below) Crowds start to sit across from St Paul's Church, designed by Inigo Jones and where street buskers regularly try their luck with the ever constant flow of visitors to Covent Garden

Veolia, a multinational utility services company, is contracted by the City of Westminster to handle its rubbish, ensuring disposal is achieved in an economic and environmentally sustainable manner – given the reality of clearing over the 200,000 tonnes

(Above) One of the 200 vehicles and machines employed in Westminster begins one of three daily collections in Chinatown

(Top right) Pavements are washed regularly

(Below) The streets are swept at the same time

(Below) The collection of plastic sacks begins in Chinatown with the hand-pulled trolley

(Overleaf) Each area of Westminster is cleaned by the same regular team, creating a sense of communal involvement. Here, some of the workers and their managers are reflected in the freshly washed Piccadilly Circus

of waste generated, and sweeping a total of 8,400 kilometres of street, every week. As a result, Veolia operate a unique 24 hours a day, seven days a week service – which includes working on Christmas Day.

(Above) Defying the mighty roar of London's traffic, the channel around Eros gets swept

(Below) Ravi Kumar is one of 75 inspectors employed by the City of Westminster to check that relevant environmental legislation, by-laws and statutes are abided by. Pavements are clear, street hawkers are licensed, rubbish is disposed of properly and a myriad of other regulations that ensure a civilized space. Here he checks whether a sign is blocking the pavement

9

The many hundreds of restaurants, clubs, bars, pubs, hotels, guest houses and even old fashioned bed and breakfast establishments which crowd around the City of Westminster cover a range and diversity equal to any city anywhere in the world.

André Balazs, outside the Chiltern Firehouse, in Marylebone, a 126-seat restaurant and 26-room hotel, which opened in 2013. He told the *Wall Street Journal* he was heavily influenced by his idol, the Swiss hotelier César Ritz, thought to be the first to mist fragrances into his hotels. 'For the muscular Firehouse, Balazs chose a scent with notes of leather and tea,' the newspaper informed its readers

Sitting in a corner of the Ivy, Richard Caring is Chairman, and Lilly Newell is executive director, of Caprice Holdings and the Birley Group of clubs. The group is expanding, with other Ivy branches in Covent Garden, Marylebone, St John's Wood and Dubai

(Above) Oliver Peyton in the Member's Bar at the Royal Academy. His company, Peyton & Byrne, run two restaurants in the Royal Academy as well as venues at the National Gallery, the Institute of Contemporary Arts, the Wallace Collection and the British Library. They have six bakery shops in prime locations like Covent Garden and delicious cakes can be collected after any online order has been placed

(Below) Ai Weiwei's *Trees* installation in the Courtyard in front of Burlington House, home of the Royal Academy since 1867

(Above) St John's Wood can boast one of the few restaurants left in London, built into a residential block. This one was built in 1938 and has only one-bedroomed apartments, though each one has a balcony

(Overleaf) Just across from Regent's Park, Oslo Court is surrounded by apartment blocks. St John's Wood has been a highly desirable residential part of Westminster since the 19th century

(Right) The restaurant has been run by the same family since 1982, though Neil, the legendary dessert waiter, worked here for the restaurant's previous owners

10

The City of Westminster has eleven lending libraries, sharing over 1 million volumes available for home loan. Other resources such as DVDs, CDs, games, language courses and talking books are also available. All the branches stock newspapers, magazines and can provide local information. There are several specialist libraries that are available to all library members, including the Westminster Music Library, the Westminster Chinese Library and the Westminster Archives and Local Studies Centre. The Central Reference Library and Marylebone Library are the two reference libraries and each have their own specialist subjects and they also have extensive resources to help with general enquires.

The Church Street branch's entrance is behind the busy 6-days-a-week market

The branch is surrounded by flats and maisonettes that form part of the extensive Church Street Estate

(Top) There are two
levels...

(Middle) An activities area
awaiting the children...

(Bottom) The Fiction area
awaiting readers...

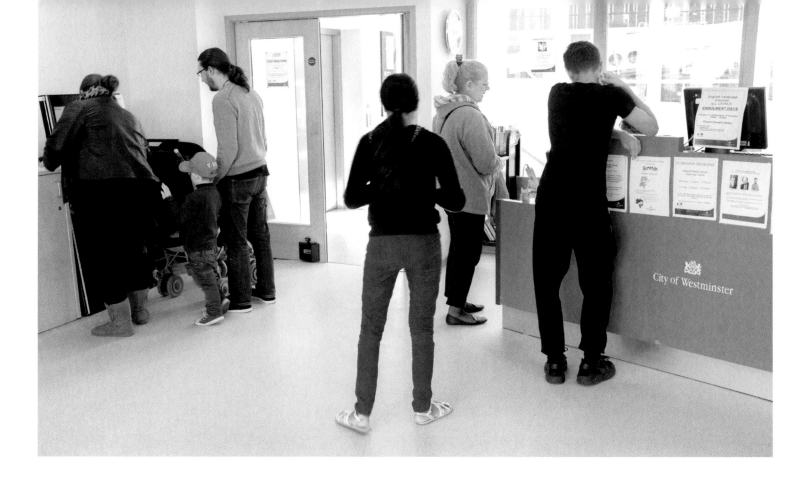

(Above) Books come back and go out and questions are answered at the main desk

(Below) The Central Reference Library is a stone's throw from the back of Shakespeare's statue, overlooking the ever-bustling Leicester Square

(Left) The Central Reference Library is housed in what was once the residence of Sir Isaac Newton, who lived there from 1710 until 1727. It was also the house of Dr Charles Burney and his daughter, Fanny. The original site was a chapel built for the Huguenots in 1693

This is a specialist public reference library with regular and varied events, an exhibition space and a business information point. There are also three reading rooms available for reading and study

11

Churchill Gardens, a large housing estate in Pimlico, was developed between 1946 and 1962 replacing houses extensively damaged during the Blitz. Comprising 1,875 homes in 40 blocks, the estate is notable as the only housing project completed under the ambitious Greater London Plan of 1944, developed by the town planner, Sir Leslie Abercrombie.

A pioneering example, it acted as a model for many subsequent public housing projects

(Above, from left to right) Jonathan Cowie, CEO CityWest Homes, Mr & Mrs Morris, long-term residents (their 55th wedding anniversary was to be celebrated the day after this picture was taken) and Liam Beecham, estates manager, based on Churchill Gardens estate

Churchill Gardens was designated a conservation area in 1990 and in 1998, six blocks were Grade II listed

Westminster has direct responsibility for the 42 primary schools and 11 secondary schools which provide education for the children of the City's residents.

Gateway Primary School serves the children and families of the Lisson Grove and Church Street areas of Westminster. It has just over 700 children, and its last Ofsted Report quoted a parent as saying: 'Gateway is an "exceptional school", echoing the views of many. This view endorses the school's accurate evaluation of its work and the inspection judgement of outstanding'

(Below) A First-year phonetic lesson gets underway

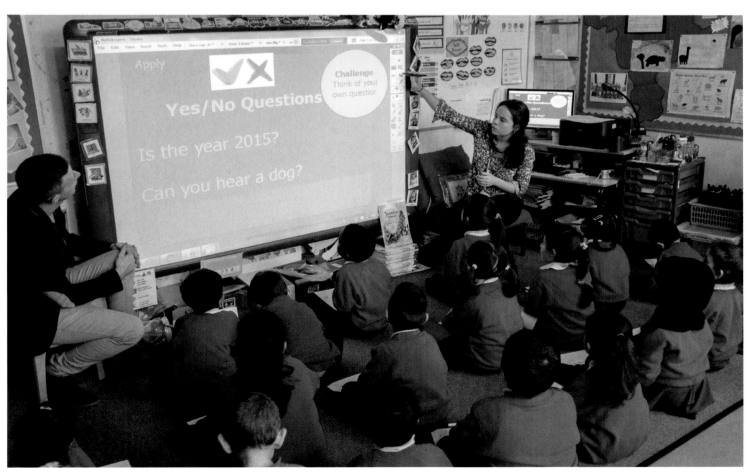

An experiment in a Year 7 science lesson goes well

Pimlico Academy is a mixed secondary school for pupils aged 11-19 from the South of Westminster. There are over 1,200 children and Ofsted rated it 'outstanding'

Professor Geoff Petts has been Vice-Chancellor of the University of Westminster since 2007. He studied physical geography and geology at the University of Liverpool and gained his PhD at the University of Southampton. Appointed a lectureship at Loughborough University in 1979, a chair in 1989, he became head of department in 1991. In 1994 he moved to the University of Birmingham, becoming Pro Vice-Chancellor, before taking up his appointment at Westminster. He is photographed in the Regent St Cinema

The University of Westminster will help establish the Sir Simon Milton Westminster University Technical College, close to Victoria. Opening in September 2017, the new UTC will offer academic and technical education in engineering and construction.

The ground-breaking ceremony took place in March 2016 with the Lord Mayor of Westminster, Cllr. The Lady Flight, Cllr. Robert Davis MBE DL and Sir Peter Rogers who are all Trustees of the Sir Simon Milton Foundation. Professor Petts stands on the left of the picture

145

(Above) An artist's impression of the Sir Simon Milton Westminster UTC. It will open in September 2017 in Pimlico. A flagship for technical skills education, it will offer 550 young people between 14 and 19 the opportunity to join a new generation of engineers, designers, technicians and project managers to build Britain's infrastructure. It will be the only central London UTC and the whole of London is in its catchment area

(Below) Karen Barker, Principal of the Sir Simon Milton Westminster UTC, photographed in October 2016 'on site', near where the ground-breaking ceremony was performed (see page 145). Karen graduated with a BSc (Hons) in Physics from the University of Manchester, and qualified as a teacher with a PGCE from St Martin's College. Her professional career began as a science journalist, prior to moving into teaching

12

A Business Improvement District (BID) is a geographical area in which the local businesses have voted to invest together to improve their environment. There are seven occupier Business Improvement Districts currently operating in Westminster.

Photographed in Oxford Street with the Christmas lights behind him, Sir Peter Rogers is the Chairman of the New West End Company, one of the largest BIDs in Europe. He was the founding Chairman of the Sir Simon Milton Foundation

Ruth Duston, Executive Director of both the Northbank and the Victoria BID, photographed on Waterloo Bridge with the Embankment, the Northbank's southern boundary, behind her

(Right) Just in the West End alone, it is estimated that when Crossrail opens, annual retail sales will reach £10 billion pounds by 2019. The department stores are one of the main reasons for the half million visitors who enter the West End every day through its 6 underground stations. Sue West is the Director of Operations at Selfridges and a member of the Strategic Board of the New West End Company. She stands in front of a plaque outside the main entrance on Oxford Street which celebrates the centenary of the store's creation in 1909

(Below) Annie Walker is Director of the Regent Street Association, representing the retailers, restaurants, offices and other businesses in the area, promoting Regent Street to both the UK and abroad. Jace Tyrrell is CEO of the New West End Company *(see page 147)*. Far below them, Regent Street bustles on

148

Since 1875, Liberty has maintained its reputation for fine design with special emphasis on the exotic from around the world. The mock-Tudor building at the side of Regent Street, built in 1924, constructed from the timbers of HMS *Impregnable* and HMS *Hindustan*, remains a tourist delight. The florist Wild at Heart creates cascades of flowers outside the Great Marlborough Street entrance

Built across from the Royal Academy, Fortnum and Mason was founded in 1707 when Hugh Mason met William Fortnum and began a business partly based on the sale of unfinished wax candles from the Royal Household, where Fortnum was footman to Queen Anne. The Piccadilly store dates back to 1840 where it was one of the first to have plate glass windows lit by gas. Fortnum and Mason was also the first shop to sell tins of Heinz baked beans in the United Kingdom

Further down Piccadilly, a Burlington Arcade Beadle keeps watch at the entrance to Lord George Cavendish's real estate development, opened in 1819. The younger brother of the Duke of Devonshire, he lived next door in Burlington House. The first Burlington Arcade Beagles were former members of his regiment, the 10th Hussars (now, following amalgamation, part of the King's Royal Hussars)

The Royal Academy attracted art dealers and auction houses to gather in the streets nearby. Reflected in the window of a gallery specialising in Dutch and Flemish old masters, other galleries offer tempting fare from far and wide

Some of the paintings to be auctioned in a sale which eventually garnered over £2 million: one of around 350 auctions held each year by the company founded in 1766 by James Christie

Westminster can still boast specialist areas of retail interest and here, in Cecil Court, antiquarian and second-hand booksellers ply their specialist trade. Still owned by the aristocratic Cecil family, booksellers have been here since before the First World War

中國太平

盛世中華美月月同輝千年傳文脈

四海太平天人共享萬古振金聲

(Above) There are now three arches around the Gerrard Street area signifying the entrances to London's Chinatown. This one, the largest, was opened by HRH The Duke of York in 2016

(Left) A window, full with Chinese food, on the corner of Gerrard Street

151

(Above) Westminster has six street markets and Church Street is its largest, occupying half the length of the street on weekdays and all of it on Saturdays

(Right) Opening in 1979, opposite the market stall where the family business started just after the Second World War, Joel & Son can now boast a Royal Warrant

(Below) A normal busy Saturday

13

As well as Soho's long involvement with the media industry, Westminster has also been home to two of the nation's broadcasting institutions, both housed in iconic buildings.

Broadcasting House, the headquarters of the BBC, stands at the tip of Regent Street, in Langham Place. Designed in Art Deco style, the building was officially opened on 15 May 1932. As part of a major consolidation of the BBC's property portfolio in London, Broadcasting House has been extensively renovated and extended. This involved the demolition of post-war extensions on the eastern side of the building, replaced by a new wing completed in 2005. The main building was refurbished, and an extension built to the rear which includes a new combined newsroom for the entire BBC News activities. Formally opened by The Queen in June 2013 the building is now home to more than 30 domestic and World Service radio stations, three 24-hour TV news channels, all of the BBC's main news bulletins and is the workplace for 6,000 BBC staff from the BBC's television, radio, news and online services

The *Breathing Sculpture* on the new wing of Broadcasting House remembers those men and women who were murdered or lost their lives in acts of war while working on behalf of the BBC. The statue of *Prospero and Ariel* was one of a number of reliefs by Eric Gill, commissioned for the original building. Ariel has always been a contentious representation since his very first appearance. The controversy over aspects of his nakedness continues today

(Above) These distinctive purpose-built headquarters of Channel 4 at 124 Horseferry Road were opened in 1994. Designed by Richard Rogers Partnership with structural engineering by Ove Arup & Partners, its 15,000 square metres has twin-storey office blocks arranged in an L shape, connected by a curved front with a concave glazed wall

The Big 4 is a 50-foot-tall statue of the Channel 4 logo which was constructed outside the building. The metal frames form the image only when viewed at a particular angle

(Right) The unassuming Edwardian villa just past the Abbey Road zebra crossing, with the white wall, has been the venue for some extraordinary events. Launched in 1931 as the principal recording studio for the Gramophone Company, Sir Edward Elgar conducted the London Symphony Orchestra at the opening ceremony and went on to record nearly all his symphonic works there. The studios are best known as the venue where the Beatles recorded most of their albums, including *Abbey Road* with its cover of the four on the zebra crossing

(Above) A constant stream of Beatle devotees risk life and limb to be photographed where their idols walked. The zebra crossing has been granted a Grade II Listed Building status by English Heritage

(Below) Graffiti left by Beatle pilgrims runs all along the wall outside the building. It is regularly whitewashed over every two months to let this never-ending poem self-perpetuate

(Overleaf) Within hours of the announcement of his death David Bowie fans began to leave tributes in front of the steps in Heddon Street where Ziggy Stardust was photographed in 1972. The plaque had been unveiled in 2012, though the street had been transformed into a pedestrianised restaurant space, rather than the dim back-alley it was when the legendary record cover was photographed there

(Right and bottom left) The end of the year is a special time in Westminster with street decorations and the erection of the fir tree in Trafalgar Square, given by the people of Norway

(Bottom right) Even after Christmas, Carnaby Street still parties on

(Left) And the Piccadilly Circus lights never fade

(Bottom and top right) Just after Christmas, the arts company Lumiere were asked to bring their own spectacular light display to the West End and over 100,000 people came to see them. Here, two installations in Regent Street amaze the crowds

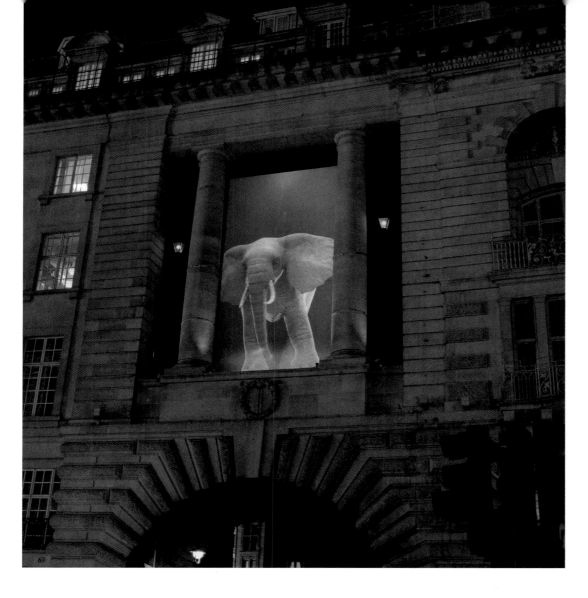

(Below) With the end of an old year and the celebration of the new, there is always a danger that overzealous revellers might choose to clamber up the delicate memorial at the heart of Piccadilly and so Eros is given a preventive wrap around. Its ever protective City Council can also wish seasonal greetings along the way

14

In his final month as London's Mayor, Boris Johnson unveiled a new statue, sculpted by Philip Jackson, which depicts Sir Simon Milton gazing at City Hall and the River Thames across Potters Fields Park, towards the Tower of London. The stature was installed at the entrance to Crown Square, part of the One Tower Bridge development by Berkeley Homes.

(Right) Recognising his significance in London, Sir Simon Milton now has a number of public memorials, including a statue by Bruce Denny at Paddington Basin *(page 17)*, a bust at Westminster City Hall *(dedication, page 5)* and another depiction of his image as part of a decorative frieze in Eagle Place, Piccadilly *(acknowledgements page, 162)*

(Left) Rt. Hon. Boris Johnson MP and Cllr. Robert Davis MBE DL reveal the finished art work

(Bottom) Harry Lewis (Berkeley Homes), Tony Pidgley CBE (Chairman of the Berkeley Group), Rt. Hon. Boris Johnson MP, Philip Jackson (sculptor), Mrs Ruth Gross (Simon's mother), Cllr. Robert Davis MBE DL, and the Rt. Hon. Greg Clark MP

ACKNOWLEDGEMENTS

The Sir Simon Milton Foundation and Quartet Books must first thank all those people, pictured within, who gave so freely of their time and allowed us to take their portraits in their workplaces and their homes. They would also like to thank all those at Westminster City Hall who assisted with suggestions and in helping to organise many of the photographic shoots.

The Sir Simon Milton Foundation and Quartet Books are grateful for permission to use the artist's impression of the Sir Simon Milton Westminster UTC on page 146, supplied with the kind cooperation of the project's developer Westminster City Council and their development partner, Linkcity, the scheme's architect, Sheppard Robson, and the building's contractor, Bouygues Construction; and the two photographs of Sir Simon Milton on pages 8 and 162 supplied from archives kept by Westminster City Council.

The Sir Simon Milton Foundation would like to thank Naim Attallah CBE, Chairman of Quartet Books, for his support throughout this entire project.

Quartet Books would also like to thank Gemma Levine for her involvement during the initial stages of the book's creation.

The plaque underneath the freize at Eagle Place recording where Sir Simon Milton lived from 1985–1989